Schizoid in a Soci

Strategies for Balancing Solitude and Social Obligation

Schizoid Personality Disorder Workbook-Guide to
understanding and managing Schizoid Personality in social
settings.

Joann Rose Gregory

Disclaimer

The information provided in "Schizoid In A Social World: Strategies for Balancing Solitude and Social Obligations" is intended for informational purposes only. It is not a substitute for professional medical advice, diagnosis, or treatment. Always seek the advice of your healthcare provider with any questions you may have regarding a medical condition or treatment and before undertaking a new health care regimen. Never disregard professional medical advice or delay in seeking it because of something you have read in this book.

Names, characters, businesses, places, events, locales, and incidents mentioned in this publication are either products of the author's imagination or used in a fictitious manner. Any resemblance to actual persons, living or dead, or actual events is purely coincidental.

Neither the publisher nor the author shall be liable for any damages arising herefrom.

Table of Contents

Preface

In a world that constantly buzzes with social connections, bustling crowds, and seemingly endless interactions, the serenity of solitude often goes unnoticed, and sometimes, even misunderstood. For many, solitude is a fleeting moment, a brief respite. But for those with Schizoid Personality Disorder (SPD), solitude is not merely a choice; it's a deeply felt need, a sanctuary for the mind and soul.

"Schizoid In A Social World: Strategies for Balancing Solitude and Social Obligations" is born out of an earnest desire to bridge two seemingly contrasting worlds: the peaceful realm of solitude and the dynamic, demanding sphere of societal obligations. This book is not a manual but a compass, guiding those with SPD through the intricate dance of balancing their intrinsic need for solitude with the external pressures of society.

As you journey through these pages, you will find insights, stories, strategies, and most importantly, validation. The chapters are meticulously designed to provide actionable advice, case studies for relatable experiences, and gentle reminders that you are not alone in this journey.

However, this book is not exclusive to those with SPD. It's a window for friends, families, colleagues, and anyone who wishes to understand the unique challenges and desires of those who resonate with the schizoid experience.

Empathy, after all, is a powerful tool in bridging gaps and building connections, even in the realm of solitude.

In an era where being social is often equated with happiness and success, it's essential to remember that the spectrum of human experience is vast and varied. There's profound strength in understanding oneself, setting boundaries, and seeking connections on one's terms. This book is a testament to that strength.

So, whether you identify with SPD, know someone who does, or are simply curious about the myriad ways in which humans connect and disconnect, I invite you to delve into these pages. May you find understanding, hope, and a renewed appreciation for the delicate balance between solitude and society.

Here's to crafting your personal balance, understanding diverse experiences, and celebrating the myriad shades of human connection.

Warmly,

Joann Rose Gregory

Introduction

Schizoid Personality Disorder (SPD)

Schizoid Personality Disorder (SPD) is a type of personality disorder classified under Cluster A personality disorders in the Diagnostic and Statistical Manual of Mental Disorders (DSM-5). Cluster A disorders are often described as "odd or eccentric" disorders. SPD is characterized by a consistent pattern of detachment from social relationships and a restricted range of emotional expression in interpersonal settings.

Characteristics of Schizoid Personality Disorder:

1. **Emotional Detachment:** Individuals with SPD often appear indifferent to the opportunity of forming close relationships and, in fact, prefer to be in solitary roles or activities. They tend to be emotionally cold, distant, and have been described as "loners."

2. **Limited Range of Emotions:** People with this disorder typically display a limited range of emotions. They might appear aloof, uninterested, or even cold. While they can experience emotions, they often don't express them.

3. **Preference for Solitary Activities:** Those with SPD often choose hobbies and jobs that allow them to be alone. They might prefer mechanical or abstract

tasks, for instance, over those which require a lot of social interaction.

4. **Lack of Close Relationships:** Apart from immediate family, individuals with SPD often have no desire for intimate relationships or friendships. They might be indifferent to the expectations and opinions of others and do not necessarily feel a need to respond to societal pressures in conventional ways.

5. **Indifference to Praise or Criticism:** They typically aren't affected much by praise or criticism. Their internal emotional experience is often not influenced by external factors or others' perceptions.

6. **Limited Sexual Interest:** While it varies among individuals, there is often limited interest in sexual experiences with another person.

7. **Apathy:** They may seem directionless and unmotivated, with a seeming lack of clear goals or aspirations.

Possible Causes:

The exact cause of Schizoid Personality Disorder is unknown. However, it is believed to emerge from a complex interplay of genetic, environmental, and psychological factors. Childhood experiences, such as a lack of nurturing or more severe forms of neglect, might play a role in the development of this disorder.

Diagnosis and Treatment:

Diagnosis is typically based on a thorough interview, an overview of symptoms, and sometimes, a physical exam to rule out other medical conditions. Self-reports, insights from close relations, and observation of the individual's behavior also aid in the diagnostic process.

Treatment for SPD can be challenging because individuals with this disorder often believe they don't need help or therapy. However, therapy can be beneficial, especially if an individual seeks help for related issues, such as depression. Cognitive-behavioral therapy, which helps change negative thought patterns and behaviors, can be effective. Group therapy is typically not the first line of treatment due to the nature of the disorder, but some people with SPD find it beneficial.

Conclusion:

While Schizoid Personality Disorder might not be as widely recognized or discussed as other disorders, it's a genuine and challenging condition. The key is to approach individuals with SPD with understanding and patience, respecting their comfort levels while providing support where they may need it.

Chapter 1: The Schizoid Experience in a Social World

We live in a world of constant social interaction, be it face-to-face conversations, group activities, or the virtual barrage of social media updates. The societal framework suggests that being social, outgoing, and frequently interacting with others is the norm. There's an inherent expectation to participate, communicate, and belong. This norm, this mold, that society has cast is based on the assumption that individuals inherently seek connections, validations, and active participation in social engagements.

The Societal Mold

The "societal mold" is not a tangible entity but rather a set of implicit expectations. From early school days, children are encouraged to "play well with others," share, and make friends. As they grow, these lessons evolve into attending social events, participating in group activities, and networking. This mold presumes that the more socially engaged one is, the happier and more fulfilled they'll be.

Schizoid Personality Disorder (SPD) and the Social Paradigm

For individuals with Schizoid Personality Disorder, this mold isn't just a poor fit—it can be a straitjacket. People with SPD often feel detached from these social norms and may even find them perplexing. Their inherent nature leans towards solitude, introspection, and a limited desire for social interactions. While someone without SPD might feel rejuvenated after a party, someone with SPD might feel drained and overwhelmed.

Misunderstandings and Misconceptions

The disconnect between the inherent nature of those with SPD and societal expectations often leads to misunderstandings. They might be labeled as "loners," "antisocial," or "cold." Such labels, born out of ignorance, can be hurtful and further alienate individuals with SPD.

The Journey Ahead

It's important to understand that there's no right or wrong way to be. People with SPD have their own unique strengths, insights, and contributions to offer. This book aims to bridge the gap between the innate needs of those with SPD and the demands of society. Instead of pushing against the tide, we will explore ways to navigate through it, maintaining one's authenticity and well-being.

By understanding the schizoid experience deeply, and by validating its legitimacy, we hope to pave the way for a more balanced, harmonious existence for those with SPD in this predominantly social world.

Chapter 2: Recognizing and Embracing Your Need for Solitude

Solitude often carries a myriad of connotations, some negative and some positive. The hush of silence, the stillness of being alone with one's thoughts, the freedom from the barrage of external stimuli – all these attributes make solitude an oasis for some and a desert for others. Particularly for individuals with Schizoid Personality Disorder (SPD), solitude isn't merely a luxury; it is often a fundamental necessity. Understanding and embracing the need for solitude is a pivotal step towards achieving mental well-being and a balanced life for those with SPD.

The Therapeutic Aspects of Solitude

Humans, by evolutionary design, are social creatures. We bond, form communities, and derive a sense of belonging from groups. Yet, the same evolutionary process has ensured that solitude plays a crucial role in our psychological framework.

1. **Mental Restoration**: Solitude offers a break from the sensory overload that our modern lives constantly bombard us with. This break is not just from physical stimuli, but also from the emotional and cognitive loads that come with social interactions. The brain, during solitude, gets the much-needed downtime to process, restore, and rejuvenate.

2. **Enhanced Creativity**: Some of the world's most renowned artists, writers, and thinkers have often cited solitude as their muse. Away from distractions, the mind can wander, daydream, and come up with novel ideas. Solitude fosters deep thinking and lets the imagination roam free.

3. **Emotional Regulation**: Constant social interactions can sometimes be a whirlwind of emotions. Being alone provides an opportunity to understand, process, and regulate these emotions. It's a time when one can introspect on reactions, feelings, and moods, making sense of them without external influences.

The Difference Between Isolation and Solitude

The terms 'isolation' and 'solitude' are often used interchangeably, but they signify very different experiences.

1. **Isolation**: This is often an imposed state, where an individual is separated from others against their will or without a deliberate choice. Isolation can lead to feelings of loneliness, sadness, and can sometimes have negative psychological effects. It signifies a lack of connection, not out of preference, but due to circumstances.

2. **Solitude**: Solitude is a chosen state. It's the deliberate act of spending time alone to reconnect with oneself. Unlike the negative undertones of

isolation, solitude is often associated with positive psychological outcomes, such as better emotional regulation, increased empathy, and heightened self-awareness.

For someone with SPD, the distinction is crucial. What they seek is solitude – a chosen, therapeutic state of being, not the imposed loneliness of isolation.

Setting Aside Dedicated Time for Self-reflection

Self-reflection is a deep and internal dialogue with oneself. It's the process of understanding one's thoughts, emotions, and actions, and it plays a pivotal role in personal growth. For individuals with SPD, given their innate preference for introspection, self-reflection becomes even more crucial. Here's why and how one should set aside dedicated time for it:

1. **Understanding One's Needs**: SPD or not, everyone has a unique set of needs and boundaries. By reflecting, one can better understand what they are, how they evolve, and how to communicate them.

2. **Coping Mechanism**: Self-reflection allows for the processing of experiences, both good and bad. It becomes a way to make sense of the world and one's place in it, offering a coping mechanism for the challenges that life invariably throws.

3. **Scheduling Solitude**: In our fast-paced world, anything that isn't scheduled often gets overlooked. By setting aside dedicated time for self-reflection, one ensures that this essential activity isn't forgotten. Whether it's a few quiet moments in the morning, a weekly walk in the park, or even a periodic retreat away from everyday life, find what works and stick to it.

4. **Creating a Conducive Environment**: The environment plays a significant role in effective self-reflection. Find a quiet corner, perhaps with soft lighting, where you can sit with your thoughts. Some prefer the tranquility of nature, while others might opt for a cozy nook at home. The key is to be in a place where one feels safe and undisturbed.

Case Study 1: Maya - The Therapeutic Aspects of Solitude

Background: Maya, a 28-year-old software developer with SPD, often found herself overwhelmed in her bustling office space. The constant chatter, meetings, and group lunches made her feel drained.

Situation: One day, after an especially hectic team meeting, Maya felt the need to escape. She took a two-hour break and went to a nearby park. Away from the office's noise, she felt her stress levels drop. The serenity of nature and the solitude it offered made her feel rejuvenated.

Outcome: Realizing the therapeutic benefits of solitude, Maya made it a routine to spend at least an hour in the park daily. This solitary time allowed her to process her thoughts, feel more grounded, and approach her work with renewed energy.

Takeaway: Solitude can provide a restorative break, especially in environments that feel overwhelming. For someone like Maya with SPD, such breaks are not just beneficial but often essential.

Case Study 2: Alex - Isolation vs. Solitude

Background: Alex, a 35-year-old writer with SPD, always cherished his alone time. He considered it crucial for his creativity. However, after relocating to a new city for work, he found himself cut off from familiar faces.

Situation: While Alex had always enjoyed solitude, this new situation felt different. The city's unfamiliarity and lack of known faces made him feel lonely. He missed the occasional coffee with friends or the weekend family dinners.

Outcome: Alex realized that what he was experiencing was not the solitude he cherished but isolation. He decided to join a local book club. This gave him the flexibility to socialize on his terms while ensuring he wasn't completely cut off.

Takeaway: Even for those who value solitude, human connections remain vital. The key is to find a balance and ensure that chosen solitude doesn't transform into imposed isolation.

Case Study 3: Priya - Setting Time for Self-reflection

Background: Priya, a 40-year-old marketing consultant with SPD, often felt disconnected from her emotions. She was excellent at her job and interacted well with clients but felt a void within.

Situation: During a therapy session, Priya's counselor suggested she set aside some dedicated time for self-reflection. Initially skeptical, Priya decided to give it a try. Every evening, she'd sit on her balcony, away from her phone and other distractions, just reflecting on her day.

Outcome: This dedicated time became a revelation for Priya. She began to understand her reactions better, recognized patterns in her behavior, and started feeling more in tune with her emotions. This not only improved her personal well-being but also enhanced her professional interactions.

Takeaway: Setting aside time for self-reflection can be transformative. For Priya, it became a bridge connecting her external actions with her internal emotions, leading to a more harmonious existence.

These case studies underscore the significance of solitude, the nuances between solitude and isolation, and the transformative power of self-reflection. While each individual's journey is unique, such relatable experiences offer insights and validate the emotions of many, especially those with SPD.

In conclusion, solitude isn't an indictment of antisocial tendencies or a punishment. For many, especially those with SPD, it's a therapeutic necessity. Recognizing and embracing this need is not just about self-acceptance but also about ensuring one's psychological and emotional well-being. In the vast tapestry of human experiences, solitude is a thread that adds depth, color, and richness. It's time we recognized its value and gave it the place it deserves in our lives.

Chapter 3: Boundary Setting

The Cornerstone of Mental Well-being

Boundaries, both physical and emotional, delineate where one individual ends and another begins. They are akin to property lines in the realm of interpersonal relationships, ensuring that individuals don't inadvertently overstep or encroach upon another's personal space. For those with Schizoid Personality Disorder (SPD), setting and maintaining boundaries is not just a recommendation—it's a lifeline.

The Importance of Verbalizing Boundaries

Why Verbalize?

While some boundaries are universally understood, many are personal and might not align with societal norms or expectations. As a result, they need to be communicated to ensure they're respected.

1. **Clarity and Mutual Respect**: Clearly verbalizing boundaries ensures that there's no ambiguity. It allows both parties to understand the limits, fostering mutual respect.

2. **Prevents Misunderstandings**: Often, conflicts arise not from malice but from ignorance. By articulating boundaries, one reduces the risk of unintentional boundary violations.

3. **Empowerment**: There's a sense of empowerment that comes with asserting one's boundaries. It reinforces an individual's right to personal space and well-being.

Ways to Establish Boundaries Without Feeling Guilty

Guilt often emerges from societal expectations and internalized beliefs about how one "should" behave. Here's how to set boundaries without the accompanying guilt:

1. **Recognize the Validity of Your Needs**: Everyone, regardless of their personality type, has the right to their comfort and well-being. Your boundaries are a reflection of your needs and are as valid as anyone else's.

2. **Practice**: Start with small boundaries and gradually build up. Like any skill, boundary-setting improves with practice.

3. **Seek Support**: Discussing your feelings with a trusted friend or therapist can help reinforce the importance of your boundaries.

Dealing with Boundary Pushers

Despite best efforts, one might encounter individuals who intentionally or unintentionally push or disregard set boundaries.

1. **Stay Firm**: Reiterate your boundaries calmly but firmly. Remember, it's not about being confrontational but about ensuring your well-being.

2. **Limit Exposure**: If someone repeatedly violates your boundaries, it might be necessary to limit your interactions with them.

3. **Seek Mediation**: In situations where boundary pushing becomes a persistent issue, consider seeking mediation or counseling to address the issue.

Relatable Case Studies:

Case Study 1: Sara - Verbalizing Work Boundaries

Background: Sara, a graphic designer with SPD, often felt overwhelmed with last-minute requests from her team. They'd send her tasks late in the evening, expecting immediate turnarounds.

Situation: One evening, feeling particularly stressed, Sara decided she couldn't continue this way. The next day, she discussed her concerns with her team, highlighting her need for a proper work-life balance and setting a boundary for work requests beyond her official hours.

Outcome: While initially surprised, her team appreciated Sara's clarity. They started planning better, ensuring tasks were assigned during official hours.

Takeaway: Verbalizing boundaries can lead to better mutual respect and understanding.

Case Study 2: Ravi - Setting Boundaries Without Guilt

Background: Ravi, a teacher with SPD, was constantly approached by students for extra classes after school hours. Wanting to be helpful, he'd always agree, but it left him feeling drained.

Situation: Ravi realized he needed to set boundaries. He informed his students about dedicated hours for extra classes, ensuring he also had personal downtime.

Outcome: Some students initially expressed disappointment, but over time they respected Ravi's boundaries and appreciated the structured extra class hours.

Takeaway: It's possible to set boundaries and still fulfill responsibilities without feeling guilty.

Case Study 3: Leah - Handling a Boundary Pushing Friend

Background: Leah, a writer with SPD, had a friend who'd often drop by unannounced, disrupting her solitude and writing routine.

Situation: Despite hinting at her discomfort, the friend continued this behavior. Leah decided to have a direct conversation, explaining her need for solitude and structured social interactions.

Outcome: While the friend was initially defensive, over time she came to understand and respect Leah's boundaries.

Takeaway: Direct conversations, though challenging, can often resolve persistent boundary issues.

In conclusion, boundaries are vital for mental well-being, especially for individuals with SPD. By recognizing the importance of boundaries, practicing setting them, and learning to deal with boundary pushers, one can navigate interpersonal relationships with greater ease and confidence.

Chapter 4: Identifying and Understanding Your Social Limits

Recognizing Signs of Social Fatigue

Social fatigue is not merely the feeling of being tired after a long day of interaction. For individuals, especially those with Schizoid Personality Disorder (SPD), social fatigue can manifest after a brief or minimal interaction. It's the profound weariness, both mentally and emotionally, that comes from social interactions that surpass one's threshold. The subtleties of conversations, the nuances of group dynamics, and the sheer act of being present can all contribute to this fatigue.

This fatigue can manifest in various ways. Some individuals might feel an overwhelming desire to retreat, while others could experience irritability or a decline in their ability to concentrate. Often, there's a sense of being 'full' — where no more information or interaction can be processed, akin to a sponge that's saturated and cannot absorb any more water. Physical symptoms like headaches or a rapid heartbeat could also indicate that an individual is reaching their limit. Understanding these signs is crucial because it helps one take timely actions to prevent a complete drain or a possible breakdown.

Creating a Personal Social Energy Meter

The concept of a personal social energy meter is metaphorical, representing one's capacity for social interactions. Just as a car has a fuel gauge, each person has an internal gauge that reflects their social energy reserves. While the car's gauge shows the amount of fuel, the personal social energy meter displays the remaining social energy.

It's important to note that this meter is unique to each individual. What depletes it quickly for one might have a negligible effect on another. Some might find group interactions draining, while one-on-one conversations could be another's Achilles' heel. Understanding and visualizing this meter requires introspection. Regular self-check-ins can help individuals gauge where they stand on their meter, allowing them to foresee when they might run out of social energy and need a period of solitude to recharge.

Pacing Yourself in Social Situations

Recognizing one's social limits is just the first step. The next, and often more challenging step, is to ensure that you don't push yourself beyond these limits. This is where pacing becomes crucial.

Imagine running a marathon. A runner understands that sprinting right at the start could exhaust them prematurely. Instead, they pace themselves, ensuring they have enough energy to complete the race. Social interactions, especially for someone with SPD, can be visualized similarly. Instead of diving deep into a social marathon, it's wise to take measured steps, interspersing interactions with moments of rest or solitude.

For instance, if an individual knows they have a socially demanding event in the evening, they could ensure some quiet time before the event to start on a full meter. Similarly, planning a period of solitude after the event can help in recharging. Pacing can also mean setting time limits on interactions or ensuring there are short breaks during prolonged events.

Case Study 1: Sam - Navigating Workplace Socials

Background:
Sam, a diligent accountant with SPD, loved his job because it allowed him pockets of solitary work. However, the monthly team dinners were a challenge. They were loud, prolonged, and left Sam feeling completely drained.

Situation:
One evening, after particularly grueling team festivities, Sam found himself unable to focus on work for the next two days. He recognized that these social gatherings were pushing him beyond his limits.

Outcome:
Sam decided to discuss his feelings with his manager. He explained his need for solitude and how these events affected his productivity. Together, they worked out a

compromise: Sam would attend the dinners but would leave earlier than others. Furthermore, Sam started practicing a routine of taking a short walk midway during the event to recharge.

Takeaway:
Understanding and communicating one's social limits can lead to supportive solutions. Sam didn't avoid his social responsibility but found a way to manage it without exhausting himself.

Case Study 2: Aisha - The Weekend Retreat

Background:
Aisha, a freelance photographer with SPD, had a close-knit group of college friends. Every year, they planned a weekend retreat. While Aisha cherished these reunions, the idea of two days of continuous social interaction was daunting.

Situation:
During one such retreat, Aisha felt overwhelmed by the constant chatter and group activities. She felt her social energy meter depleting rapidly and was on the verge of a breakdown.

Outcome:
Aisha decided to pace herself. She began taking short

breaks, retreating to her room to read or listen to music. She also communicated her feelings to her friends, explaining her need for these solitary breaks. To her surprise, not only were her friends understanding, but some even confessed that they too felt the need for occasional breaks.

Takeaway:
Pacing oneself and establishing periodic respites during intense social situations can be beneficial. Often, open communication can lead to greater understanding and even reveal shared feelings among peers.

Case Study 3: Leo - Daily Commute Ritual

Background:
Leo, a librarian with SPD, had a daily train commute of one hour each way. The crowded train, with its cacophony of conversations and proximity to strangers, started affecting Leo's mood and energy levels.

Situation:
Leo dreaded his commutes. He would arrive at work already feeling socially fatigued, and by the time he reached home, he felt completely drained, leaving no energy for family interactions.

Outcome:
Leo decided to change his approach. He started carrying noise-canceling headphones and immersing himself in audiobooks during the commute. This created a bubble of solitude for him amidst the crowd. By making this small

change, Leo transformed a draining experience into a recharging one.

Takeaway:
Even in unavoidable social situations, there are ways to find pockets of solitude. For Leo, the headphones and audiobooks became tools to recharge his social energy meter, allowing him to maintain his balance throughout the day.

Each of these case studies underscores the importance of recognizing, respecting, and responding to one's social limits. By implementing strategies tailored to their unique needs, individuals can find ways to thrive in social environments without compromising their well-being.

Understanding your social limits and learning to pace yourself is akin to mastering the art of balancing. It's about ensuring that the scales never tip too much on one side, maintaining an equilibrium that prioritizes mental well-being. For individuals with SPD, this mastery can be the difference between thriving in a social world and merely surviving in it.

Chapter 5: Building Meaningful Connections on Your Terms

The human journey, for many, is marked by connections. These connections are the threads that weave the fabric of our lives, bringing color, depth, and texture. However, for individuals with Schizoid Personality Disorder (SPD), traditional avenues of connecting can feel overwhelming or inauthentic. But does this mean they should forsake connections altogether? Not at all. Instead, it's about redefining what connection means and finding ways to build these bonds on their terms.

Finding Your Tribe: Connecting with Like-minded Individuals

We live in a vast world, but within this expanse, there exist pockets of individuals who resonate with our wavelength. Finding this tribe is like coming home. It's about seeking those who understand your silences as much as your words. For those with SPD, this tribe might be others who appreciate depth over breadth, who value quality over quantity, and who understand the sanctity of personal space. Joining clubs, attending workshops, or participating in activities that align with one's interests can be gateways to discovering these like-minded souls. The beauty of such connections is that they don't demand transformation; instead, they celebrate authenticity.

The Value of One-on-One Interactions

While large groups can be draining, one-on-one interactions can be transformative. These interactions offer depth and intimacy. They allow conversations to flow seamlessly, from the mundane to the profound. For someone with SPD, this setting can be a comfortable arena to connect. It provides the space to listen and be heard without the distractions of group dynamics. It also ensures that the interaction remains paced, offering the opportunity to delve deep without feeling overwhelmed.

Using Technology to Facilitate Comfortable Interactions

Technology, in many ways, has been a boon for those seeking alternative modes of connection. Platforms like video calls, chat applications, and online forums offer a bridge to connect while still retaining a layer of comfortable distance. These tools allow individuals with SPD to control the intensity and duration of interactions. They also provide the flexibility of asynchronous communication—responding when one feels ready, rather than in the immediacy of the moment. In this digital age, technology serves as a conduit, ensuring that distance no longer impedes connection.

Relatable Case Studies:

Case Study 1: Maya - Discovering Her Book Club

Background:
Maya, a literature enthusiast with SPD, often felt out of place at large social gatherings. However, her love for books was a passion she wanted to share.

Situation:
On a friend's recommendation, Maya decided to join a local book club. The intimate group size and focused discussions on literature made the setting comfortable for her.

Outcome:
Over time, Maya formed deep connections with fellow book lovers. The shared passion for reading and the structured format of the club allowed her to connect without feeling overwhelmed.

Takeaway:
Shared interests can be a gateway to finding one's tribe, allowing for connections built on mutual passion and understanding.

Case Study 2: Ethan - The Coffee Shop Conversations

Background:
Ethan, a researcher with SPD, often felt drained in group meetings. However, he cherished the deep conversations he had with his colleague, Zoe, over coffee.

Situation:
Recognizing the value of these one-on-one interactions, Ethan began scheduling regular coffee breaks with Zoe. These sessions became an oasis of meaningful connection amidst his otherwise hectic routine.

Outcome:
The coffee shop conversations deepened Ethan's bond

with Zoe. They discussed everything, from research to life philosophies, and Ethan found these interactions rejuvenating.

Takeaway:
One-on-one interactions can offer depth and intimacy, allowing for profound connections that might be elusive in larger settings.

Case Study 3: Olivia - Embracing Digital Pen Pals

Background:
Olivia, a writer with SPD, loved connecting with people but found face-to-face interactions exhausting.

Situation:
Olivia stumbled upon a digital pen pal platform. She began exchanging long, thoughtful emails with individuals from around the world.

Outcome:
The asynchronous nature of email allowed Olivia to connect on her terms. She formed deep, meaningful relationships, all from the comfort of her home.

Takeaway:
Technology offers avenues to connect that respect individual preferences, ensuring that the essence of connection is retained without the associated discomfort.

Building connections on one's terms is not about isolation but about authenticity. It's about understanding one's own needs and finding avenues that respect and reflect these needs. In doing so, individuals, even those with SPD, can find their tapestry of connections, woven with threads that resonate with their unique rhythm.

Chapter 6: Practical Tips for Navigating Social Events

In a world where social interactions form the bedrock of personal and professional life, avoiding them altogether is neither practical nor often desirable. While for many, social events are the highlight of their week or month, for individuals with Schizoid Personality Disorder (SPD), they can pose significant challenges. The cacophony of voices, the often unspoken social expectations, and the sheer energy required to navigate these can be draining. However, with a few strategies in place, these events can become more manageable, if not entirely enjoyable.

The "Exit Strategy": Planning Ahead for Graceful Departures

Every attendee at a social event has their own comfort level in terms of duration and engagement. For individuals with SPD, this comfort level might be on the shorter end. Recognizing this, it's pivotal to have an exit strategy. This isn't about running away or making covert escapes but about ensuring one's well-being while being respectful to others. By letting the host or a few close attendees know in advance about potential early departure, it offers a way to leave without causing undue concern or drawing unnecessary attention. This strategy provides an assurance, a mental note, that when things get too overwhelming, there is a way out. Such a plan can often make the difference between attending an event with dread or with a semblance of control.

Engaging in Selective Participation

A social event is usually a mix of various activities, conversations, and group dynamics. Not every aspect of it might resonate with an individual's comfort zone. Engaging in selective participation is about finding pockets within the event that align more closely with one's interests and comfort levels. For instance, if a large group discussion feels overwhelming, maybe a side conversation with one or two individuals about a shared interest might be more palatable. Or if a dance floor isn't enticing, perhaps a quiet corner with a book or observing a game might be. The idea is to be present, to participate, but in ways that honor one's own boundaries.

Pre-event Preparations to Minimize Stress

Anticipation, they say, is often worse than the event itself. The build-up, the mounting anxiety, and the endless what-ifs can make the actual event seem ten times more daunting. Pre-event preparations can be a way to alleviate some of this stress. This can range from simple acts like choosing comfortable clothing, ensuring one is well-rested, or even having a small meal so hunger isn't an added stressor. On a deeper level, it might involve visualizing the event, mentally preparing for certain conversations, or setting personal goals like staying for a specific duration or speaking to a certain number of people. Familiarizing oneself with the venue or the attendees, if possible, can also reduce the number of unknown variables. These preparations act as armor, equipping one to face the event not as a battlefield but as a challenge that can be navigated.

Relatable Case Studies:

Case Study: Miranda's Art Exhibition Opening

Background:
Miranda, a budding artist with SPD, had her first art exhibition opening. It was a significant milestone in her career, but the thought of interacting with a crowd, answering questions about her art, and the inevitable small talk filled her with dread.

Strategy Implementation:

- **Exit Strategy**: Miranda informed the event coordinator in advance that she might need to take regular breaks due to her nervousness. This gave her a legitimate reason to step out periodically, ensuring she had moments of reprieve.

- **Selective Participation**: Knowing that discussing her art might be overwhelming with large groups, Miranda set up a small, intimate corner where interested attendees could sit down with her for one-on-one conversations about specific pieces they were intrigued by.

- **Pre-event Preparations**: A day before the event, Miranda visited the gallery, familiarizing herself with every nook and corner. She even held a mock Q&A with a close friend, preparing herself for potential questions.

Outcome:
The event was a success. Many attendees appreciated the personal touch of Miranda's intimate corner. When conversations became too much, she'd politely excuse herself, citing her earlier communicated reason. The exhibition was not only a testament to her artistic prowess but also her ability to manage her social boundaries effectively.

Case Study: Raj's College Reunion

Background:
Raj, an introverted software developer diagnosed with SPD, received an invitation to his 10-year college reunion. The thought of revisiting old memories was enticing, but the idea of mingling with forgotten faces was intimidating.

Strategy Implementation:

- **Exit Strategy**: Raj informed a few close college buddies that he might not stay for the entire duration. He also set a personal timeframe: he'd leave after dinner, before the after-party started.

- **Selective Participation**: Instead of drifting aimlessly, Raj decided to stick with his close-knit group. They reminisced, shared recent life updates, and occasionally joined larger groups. Raj felt comfortable, shielded by familiar faces.

- **Pre-event Preparations**: Raj reached out to a few alumni beforehand, catching up and gauging who all would attend. On the day of the reunion, he wore his favorite comfortable outfit and carried a pocketbook, giving him an excuse to step aside when he needed a break.

Outcome:
Raj enjoyed the reunion more than he had anticipated. By setting clear boundaries and selectively participating, he was able to reconnect with old friends without feeling overwhelmed. He left after dinner, as planned, on a positive note.

These case studies highlight that with careful planning and understanding one's own boundaries, individuals with SPD can navigate social situations in ways that honor their comfort levels while also allowing for meaningful interactions.

In conclusion, while social events can be daunting, they are also an intrinsic part of our societal fabric. With the right strategies, even those with SPD can find ways to engage with them on their terms, ensuring their well-being while also fulfilling societal expectations.

Chapter 7: Workplace Strategies for the Schizoid Individual

The modern workplace, with its open spaces, collaborative projects, and team-building activities, can often be challenging terrain for the schizoid individual. For those with Schizoid Personality Disorder (SPD), the constant interaction, coupled with the inherent expectations of conformity, can be not just draining but sometimes profoundly stressful. Recognizing these challenges, it's vital to equip oneself with strategies to navigate the work environment while maintaining personal well-being.

Negotiating for Personal Space and Remote Work

Personal space, both physical and metaphorical, is essential for someone with SPD. The advent of remote working has been a boon for many such individuals. However, not all roles or companies readily offer this flexibility. For someone with SPD, it might be beneficial to open a dialogue with HR or superiors about the possibility of partial or full remote work. This conversation should not just revolve around personal comfort but also focus on productivity. Often, a quiet, personal space can lead to enhanced focus and efficiency, a win-win for both the employee and the employer. In scenarios where remote work isn't feasible, simple adjustments like providing a secluded workstation or allowing for periodic breaks can go a long way in ensuring mental comfort.

Managing Group Projects and Team Dynamics

Collaboration is often the key in many modern workplaces. Group projects, team meetings, and brainstorming sessions are all integral parts of organizational dynamics. For an individual with SPD, these can be sources of anxiety. Instead of shying away, a more strategic approach can be beneficial. One can take on roles within the group that align more with one's comfort zone. For instance, instead of being the presenter, one can be the researcher or the note-taker. Ensuring clear communication with team members about one's strengths and comfort areas can lead to a more harmonious group dynamic. Additionally, utilizing digital communication tools can sometimes be a less stressful way to convey ideas and provide updates.

Seeking Understanding from Superiors about Your Unique Needs

Transparency is often underappreciated. While it's not necessary, or sometimes even advisable, to divulge one's diagnosis, communicating one's unique working style and needs can be beneficial. This could mean discussing preferred communication methods, the ideal environment for peak productivity, or even periodic needs for solitude. Most superiors value productivity and results over conforming to a specific working style. By ensuring that one's unique needs don't hinder the end goals, and might in fact enhance them, a more understanding and flexible work environment can be negotiated.

Relatable Case Studies:

Case Study: Elena's Transition to Remote Work

Background:
Elena, a content strategist with a leading tech firm and diagnosed with SPD, found the daily hustle of office life taxing. The open-floor plan, team lunches, and regular meetings were increasingly becoming sources of anxiety.

The Journey:
Elena decided to approach her superiors with a proposal to work remotely. She presented data highlighting how her most productive days were those when she worked from home. By showcasing her ability to deliver quality work on time, consistently, she made a case for her remote work not being a matter of personal comfort but an avenue for enhanced productivity.

Outcome:
Elena's superiors, seeing the merit in her arguments, agreed to a trial period. Three months in, Elena's productivity had indeed improved, and she felt more at ease, balancing team meetings with focused work sessions from her home office. Recognizing the benefits, her firm allowed her a flexible work arrangement, setting a precedent for others who might need similar accommodations.

Case Study: Liam's Role in Group Projects

Background:

Liam, a software developer with SPD, loved his job but dreaded group projects. The dynamics of team interactions, coupled with brainstorming sessions, left him feeling overwhelmed.

The Journey:

Instead of avoiding these projects, Liam began volunteering for roles that suited his strengths and comfort zones. He took up responsibilities like coding, documentation, and data analysis, roles that required minimal interactions. When group discussions were essential, he'd communicate his ideas via emails or shared documents, ensuring his voice was heard without the traditional face-to-face interactions.

Outcome:

Liam's team began to recognize and appreciate his unique working style. They saw that his contributions, though not always vocal, were vital to the project's success. Over time, the team found a rhythm where Liam's strengths were leveraged without pushing him into uncomfortable social situations.

Case Study: Naomi's Conversation with Her Superior

Background:

Naomi, a financial analyst with SPD, found the constant barrage of meetings and impromptu discussions with her manager draining. While she valued feedback, the frequent interactions left her feeling perpetually on edge.

The Journey:
Naomi scheduled a meeting with her manager. In the discussion, she highlighted her commitment to her role and her appreciation for the feedback. However, she also communicated her preference for structured interactions, perhaps in the form of weekly or bi-weekly reviews, instead of daily check-ins.

Outcome:
Naomi's manager, recognizing her dedication and valuing her comfort, agreed to the proposal. The structured interactions ensured that Naomi received the necessary feedback without feeling overwhelmed. Over time, this not only improved Naomi's mental well-being but also the quality of her work.

These case studies emphasize the importance of communication, self-awareness, and leveraging one's strengths in the workplace. For individuals with SPD, with the right strategies and understanding superiors and teammates, the work environment can be tailored to suit their unique needs without compromising on productivity or team goals.

In conclusion, the workplace, with its inherent dynamics, doesn't have to be a source of perennial stress for the schizoid individual. With open communication, strategic positioning, and a focus on results, one can carve out a niche that respects both organizational goals and personal well-being.

Chapter 8: Conclusion: Crafting Your Personal Balance

In a world that's increasingly interconnected and social, navigating the delicate balance between solitude and societal obligations becomes an art. For individuals with Schizoid Personality Disorder (SPD), this balance isn't just a preference—it's essential for mental well-being and overall happiness. Achieving this equilibrium, however, doesn't mean cutting oneself off from the world or forcing oneself into uncomfortable situations constantly. Instead, it's about understanding oneself deeply, planning around one's unique needs, and practicing a tremendous amount of self-compassion.

Understanding oneself is the first and foremost step. It involves recognizing the triggers that lead to discomfort or anxiety and acknowledging the situations where one feels at peace. Self-awareness also entails grasping the nuances of one's SPD, as the spectrum of experiences can vary from person to person. For some, a small gathering might be enjoyable, while for others, even a one-on-one interaction can be taxing. Recognizing these personal thresholds helps in anticipating challenges and preparing for them.

Once there's clarity on what one's comfort zones and boundaries are, the next step is planning. This doesn't mean having a rigid structure for every day but rather developing strategies that can be employed in different situations. For instance, if a social gathering is on the horizon, planning an exit strategy or having a trusted confidant to act as a buffer can be helpful. Similarly, in a workplace setting, negotiating for personal space or managing group dynamics becomes easier when there's a game plan in place.

Yet, all the understanding and planning won't be effective unless one practices self-compassion. Society, peers, or even family might not always understand the intricacies of SPD. There might be judgments, misconceptions, or undue pressures. In such situations, being gentle with oneself becomes paramount. It's okay to decline invitations, seek solitude, or communicate boundaries. At the same time, it's also alright to occasionally step out of one's comfort zone, knowing that it's a conscious choice and not an enforced obligation.

Crafting a personal balance in life, especially with SPD, is a journey rather than a destination. There will be days of triumph, where one feels in perfect harmony with one's surroundings, and then there might be days of struggle. The key is to keep iterating, learning from each experience, and continually striving for a balance that respects both the need for solitude and the inevitable societal obligations.

In essence, life for an individual with SPD can be rich, fulfilling, and in harmony with their inner self. With the right strategies, a touch of planning, and a heart full of compassion, one can craft a life that resonates with one's true essence, creating a beautiful balance between the inner world of solitude and the outer world of society.

References and Further reading

1. **Millon, T., & Davis, R. D.** (1996). *Disorders of personality: DSM-IV and beyond*. John Wiley & Sons.

2. **Rifkin, A.** (1981). The schizoid personality and related disorders: schizotypal, schizoaffective, and schizophreniform. *Comprehensive textbook of psychiatry/III*, 3, 1363-1376.

3. **Guntrip, H.** (1969). *Schizoid phenomena, object-relations, and the self*. International Universities Press.

4. **Klein, R.** (1995). The schizoid dilemma in the contemporary workplace. *Organizational and Social Dynamics*, 4(1), 58-75.

5. **Cain, S.** (2013). *Quiet: The power of introverts in a world that can't stop talking*. Penguin UK.

6. **Kaufman, S. B.** (2015). *Ungifted: Intelligence redefined*. Basic Books.

7. **Masterson, J. F.** (2000). *The search for the real self: Unmasking the personality disorders of our age*. Free Press.

8. **Rowe, D.** (2006). *Empathy in the treatment of schizoid deficits*. The Psychoanalytic Quarterly, 75(1), 23-50.

9. **Aron, E. N.** (2016). *The highly sensitive person: How to thrive when the world overwhelms you*. Citadel Press.

10. **Turkle, S.** (2017). *Reclaiming conversation: The power of talk in a digital age*. Penguin.

11. **Kahneman, D.** (2011). *Thinking, fast and slow*. Macmillan.

12. **Hallowell, E. M., & Ratey, J. J.** (2011). *Shine: Using brain science to get the best from your people*. Harvard Business Press.

13. **Nardi, D.** (2011). *Neuroscience of personality: Brain savvy insights for all types of people*. Radiance House.

Support groups

Support groups offer individuals facing various challenges an opportunity to share their experiences and offer mutual support. For many conditions, including mental health disorders, support groups can be found worldwide.

For Schizoid Personality Disorder and other related conditions, here are some general types of support groups and platforms where one might find relevant support:

1. **Mental Health America (MHA)**: A leading nonprofit addressing the needs of those living with mental illness in the U.S. They provide a range of resources, including links to support groups.

2. **National Alliance on Mental Illness (NAMI)**: An American-based organization that offers local support groups and educational resources for those with mental illnesses and their families.

3. **Mind**: A UK-based charity providing advice and support for anyone facing a mental health challenge. They also have links to local support groups and resources.

4. **Befrienders Worldwide**: An international network offering emotional support to prevent suicide. They provide directory listings for helplines around the world.

5. **Reddit**: There are many subreddits dedicated to mental health, where individuals share their experiences and support one another. While these aren't formal support groups, many find solace in connecting with others who face similar challenges.

6. **7 Cups**: An online platform offering emotional support through trained listeners. They also have community forums for various topics related to mental health.

7. **Meetup**: This platform facilitates the creation of local groups around various topics, including mental health support. Some individuals have organized or found local support groups tailored to specific needs.

8. **International Therapist Directory**: This directory lists mental health professionals around the world who serve the expatriate community. Many of these professionals might be aware of local support resources.

9. **Mental Health Europe**: An umbrella organization representing associations and individuals in the field of mental health in Europe. They might have resources or connections to support groups in various European countries.

10. **World Federation for Mental Health**: An international advocacy and education organization

that might have resources or information about support groups in various parts of the world.

It's essential to vet each group or platform to ensure it provides a safe and supportive environment. If you or someone you know is dealing with a specific mental health issue, it's also a good idea to reach out to local mental health organizations or professionals, as they might be aware of support groups in the area tailored to particular needs.

Printed in Great Britain
by Amazon

44101382R00030